Kid's Travel Journal

Written by:

_____

(write your name here)

Cover and page design by Jeff Sechler - Copyright © 2013

ISBN: 1490366911
ISBN-13: 978-1490366913

Printed in the U.S.A
2013 – First Edition

CONTENTS

Note: Write the destination of your trip on the line for easy reference next time you look at your journal!

More fun kid's books by the author:

ARE WE THERE YET?

Over 140 games, riddles and tongue twisters for hours of traveling fun!
ISBN: 978-1463785444

BEGINNER WORD AND
NUMBER PUZZLES FOR KIDS

Word Search, Number Search and Crossword Puzzles for kids!
ISBN: 978-1475261622

MORE BEGINNER WORD AND
NUMBER PUZZLES FOR KIDS

Even more Word Search, Number Search and Crossword Puzzles for kids!
ISBN: 978-1482384574

HOW TO USE THIS BOOK

To start, write your name on the cover using a permanent marker so that everyone knows it is yours!

Then, use this book to help make your trips even more fun. Write about your adventures and things that you did while traveling. Make a list of items you will need to take with you and of all the exciting places you want to visit. Did you do something you might want to do again? Write it down! Did you eat somewhere really fun? Write it down! Did you make a new friend on your trip? Use the space at the end of each trip to write down their name and information to keep in touch!

There are **10 days' worth of pages** for each trip. Each day provides places to write about what you did, where you went and what you liked about it.

Use it for up to 3 trips!

A NOTE TO PARENTS...

Encourage your child to take notes and write their experiences in this journal. Help them if they have any questions and be supportive of their work. Creativity is a great thing and by remembering the trip through their own experiences and feelings, they will create a memory that will truly last a lifetime.

Take a moment each day to sit down with your child and discuss how the day went in their eyes and help them to write down their thoughts. One day you will all look back on this journal and laugh and smile at the memories that were made.

Tips for getting ready for a trip.

1) Get Ready! Think about what you will need to do before leaving. Do you need someone to watch your dog? Is there anything that needs returned to the library or school? Make a list and check them off when you complete them.

2) What do I need to take along? Think about what kinds of toys, clothes or games you want to take with you. Remember that smaller items are easier to pack. So plan ahead!

3) Learn about where you are going. Use the Internet (or books) to learn more about the place you are traveling to. Make a list of interesting things and what you want to see or do. Share what you learned with the rest of your group to help them learn too!

4) Have fun! Any trip away from home can be a great adventure and a lot of fun. Be willing to try new things and do something someone else wants to do, even if it doesn't sound fun to you. You never know, you might like it!

5) Entertain yourself Take along this journal as well as some other activities to keep you busy along the way. We recommend the book *"Are We There Yet?"* which has tons of fun games to keep your whole family entertained while traveling.

What do I want to see and do on my trip?

(See page 3 for tips on what to put here.)

1) _____

2) _____

3) _____

4) _____

5) _____

6) _____

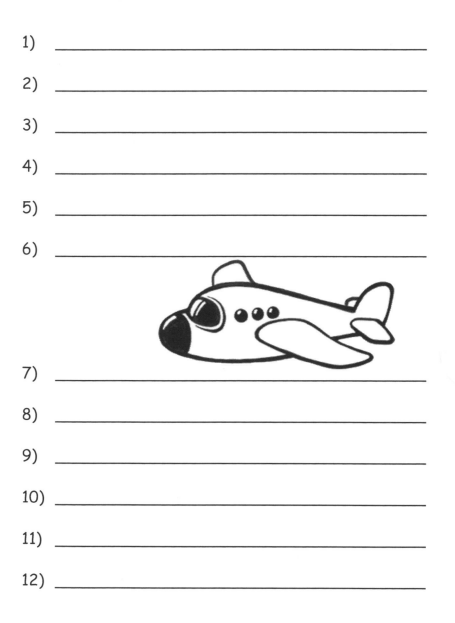

7) _____

8) _____

9) _____

10) _____

11) _____

12) _____

Who to send postcards to:

(Show them you care by sending a note!)

Post Card

Place Stamp Here

_____
_____
_____

Name: _____

Address: _____

City: _____ State _____ Zip _____

Name: _____

Address: _____

City: _____ State _____ Zip _____

Name: _____

Address: _____

City: _____ State _____ Zip _____

Name: _____

Address: _____

City: _____ State _____ Zip _____

Expectations:

Use this area to write about what you think will happen on your trip. For example, do you expect to see family, animals, waves, windmills, dinosaurs, etc. Do you think you'll have fun or go to a fun restaurant? Try to predict the future and see how things turn out!

Do this part BEFORE leaving!

_____

_____   -

_____

_____

_____

Fun facts about where I'm going:

(Write a few interesting facts about where you are going.)

1) _____

2) _____

3) _____

4) _____

5) _____

6) _____

Day 1

Today's Date: _____

What I did today: _____

_____

_____

_____

_____

What I liked best about today: _____

_____

_____

_____

NEW TO ME!

Something new I tried:_____

_____

_____

_____

Today's weather: _____

Day 1

A fun thing that happened today was:

That was fun!

_____

_____

_____

_____

A drawing about my day:

Neat things I saw today: _____

_____

_____

_____

<u>Day 2</u>

Today's Date: _____

What I did today: _____

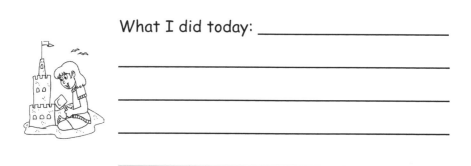

_____

_____

_____

_____

What I liked best about today: _____

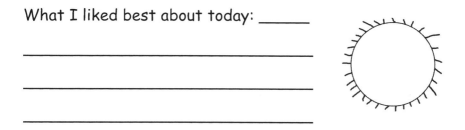

_____

_____

_____

Something new I tried:_____

NEW
TO ME!

_____

_____

_____

Today's weather: _____

Day 2

A fun thing that happened today was:

_____

_____

_____

_____

A drawing about my day:

Neat things I saw today: _____

_____

_____

_____

Day 3

Today's Date: _____

What I did today: _____
_____
_____
_____
_____

What I liked best about today: _____
_____
_____
_____

NEW

TO ME!

Something new I tried:_____
_____
_____
_____

Today's weather: _____

Day 3

A fun thing that happened today was:

_____

_____

_____

_____

A drawing about my day:

Neat things I saw today: _____

_____

_____

_____

Day 4

Today's Date: _____

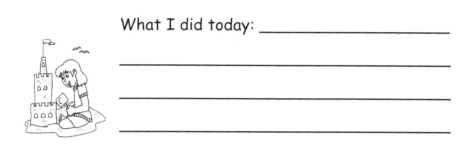

What I did today: _____

_____

_____

_____

_____

What I liked best about today: _____

_____

_____

_____

NEW
TO ME!

Something new I tried:_____

_____

_____

_____

Today's weather: _____   ## Day 4

A fun thing that happened today was:

_____

_____

_____

_____

F U N

A drawing about my day:

Neat things I saw today: _____

_____

_____

_____

Day 5

Today's Date: _____

What I did today: _____

_____

_____

_____

_____

What I liked best about today: _____

_____

_____

_____

Something new I tried:_____

NEW

TO ME!

_____

_____

_____

Today's weather: _____

Day 5

A fun thing that happened today was:

_____

_____

_____

_____

A drawing about my day:

Neat things I saw today: _____

_____

_____

_____

<u>Day 6</u>

Today's Date: _____

What I did today: _____

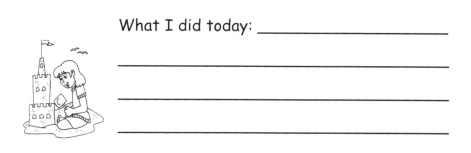

_____
_____
_____
_____

What I liked best about today: _____

_____
_____
_____

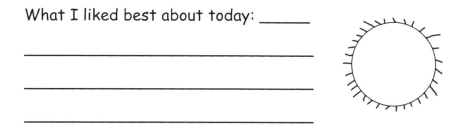

Something new I tried:_____

NEW
TO ME!

_____
_____
_____

Today's weather: _____  <u>Day 6</u>

A fun thing that happened today was:

_____

_____

_____

_____

A drawing about my day:

Neat things I saw today: _____

_____

_____

_____

Day 7

Today's Date: _____

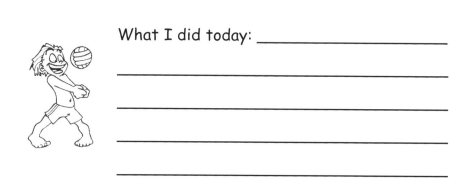

What I did today: _____

_____

_____

_____

_____

What I liked best about today: _____

_____

_____

_____

NEW

TO ME!

Something new I tried:_____

_____

_____

_____

Today's weather: _____

Day 7

A fun thing that happened today was:

_____

_____

_____

_____

A drawing about my day:

Neat things I saw today: _____

_____

_____

_____

Day 8

Today's Date: _____

What I did today: _____

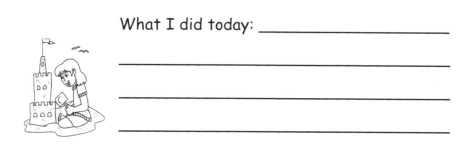

_____

_____

_____

_____

What I liked best about today: _____

_____

_____

_____

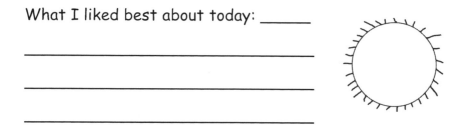

Something new I tried:_____

NEW

TO ME!

_____

_____

_____

Today's weather: _____

Day 8

A fun thing that happened today was:

_____

_____

_____

_____

A drawing about my day:

Neat things I saw today: _____

_____

_____

_____

<u>Day 9</u>

Today's Date: _____

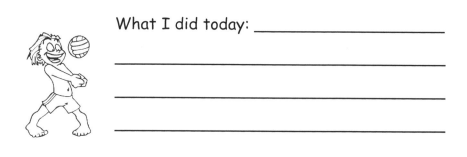

What I did today: _____

_____

_____

_____

_____

What I liked best about today: _____

_____

_____

_____

NEW TO ME!

Something new I tried:_____

_____

_____

_____

Today's weather: _____

Day 9

A fun thing that happened today was:

That was fun!

_____

_____

_____

_____

A drawing about my day:

Neat things I saw today: _____

_____

_____

_____

<u>Day 10</u>

Today's Date: _____

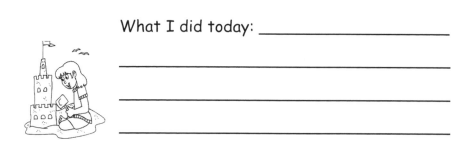

What I did today: _____

_____

_____

_____

_____

What I liked best about today: _____

_____

_____

_____

NEW

TO ME!

Something new I tried:_____

_____

— ———————————————————————

_____

Today's weather: _____  <u>Day 10</u>

A fun thing that happened today was:

_____

_____

_____

_____

A drawing about my day:

Neat things I saw today: _____

_____

_____

_____

My new friends!

(People I met while on my trip.)

Name: _____

Address: _____

City: _____ State _____ Zip _____

Email Address: _____

Phone Number: _____

Name: _____

Address: _____

City: _____ State _____ Zip _____

Email Address: _____

Phone Number: _____

Name: _____

Address: _____

City: _____ State _____ Zip _____

Email Address: _____

Phone Number: _____

Things I bought to remember this trip:

Item:	Price
_____	$ _____
_____	$ _____
_____	$ _____
_____	$ _____
_____	$ _____
_____	$ _____

Reflection:

Use this area to write anything about your trip that you didn't write down already. Did your trip go the way you expected it to? Re-read your expectations and compare.

_____

_____

_____

_____

_____

_____

_____

_____

Other memories I want to remember!

(Tape or glue tickets, photos, postcards, and other things here to remember your trip! Or you can write more about your adventures. It's up to you!)

Other memories I want to remember!

(Tape or glue tickets, photos, postcards, and other things here to remember your trip! Or you can write more about your adventures. It's up to you!)

Other memories I want to remember!

(Tape or glue tickets, photos, postcards, and other things here to remember your trip! Or you can write more about your adventures. It's up to you!)

Other memories I want to remember!

(Tape or glue tickets, photos, postcards, and other things here to remember
your trip! Or you can write more about your adventures. It's up to you!)

Other memories I want to remember!

(Tape or glue tickets, photos, postcards, and other things here to remember
your trip! Or you can write more about your adventures. It's up to you!)

<u>Trip #2</u>

My trip to

_____

(Write where you went here.)

Date: _____

(When did you go?)

Preparing for my trip

Where am I going?

_____

(Are you going to the beach, grandma's house, amusement park?)

How am I getting there?

_____

(Are you going by car, airplane, train, or boat?)

How far away is it?

_____

(How many miles is it from your home to your destination?)

Who is going?

_____

(Is your brother going along? What about mom, dad, grandma, or a friend?)

What I need to do before I leave:

(See page 3 for tips on what to put here. Check the box when you have completed or taken care of that item.)

☐ _____

☐ _____

☐ _____

☐ _____

☐ _____

☐ _____

☐ _____

☐ _____

☐ _____

☐ _____

☐ _____

☐ _____

☐ _____

☐ _____

Things I want to take with me:

(See page 3 for tips on what to put here. Check the box beside each item
after it is packed. Don't forget your toothbrush!)

☐ _____

☐ _____

☐ _____

☐ _____

☐ _____

☐ _____

☐ _____

☐ _____

☐ _____

☐ _____

☐ _____

☐ _____

☐ _____

What do I want to see and do on my trip?

(See page 3 for tips on what to put here.)

1) _____

2) _____

3) _____

4) _____

5) _____

6) _____

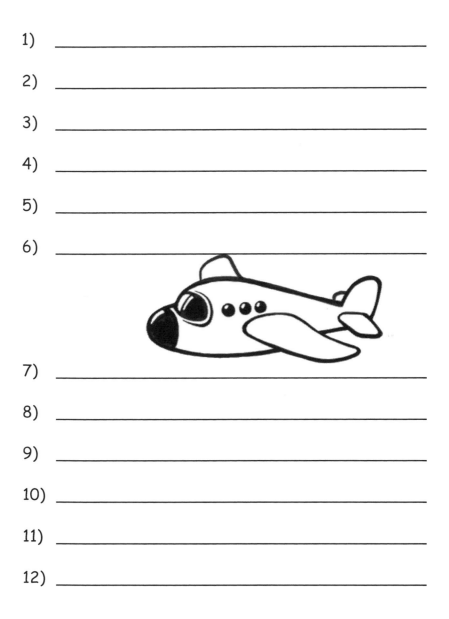

7) _____

8) _____

9) _____

10) _____

11) _____

12) _____

Who to send postcards to:

(Show them you care by sending a note!)

Post Card

Place
Stamp
Here

_____
_____
_____

Name: _____

Address: _____

City: _____ State _____ Zip _____

Name: _____

Address: _____

City: _____ State _____ Zip _____

Name: _____

Address: _____

City: _____ State _____ Zip _____

Name: _____

Address: _____

City: _____ State _____ Zip _____

Expectations:

Use this area to write about what you think will happen on your trip. For example, do you expect to see family, animals, waves, windmills, dinosaurs, etc. Do you think you'll have fun or go to a fun restaurant? Try to predict the future and see how things turn out!

Do this part BEFORE leaving!

_____

_____

_____

_____

_____

Fun facts about where I'm going:

(Write a few interesting facts about where you are going.)

7) _____

8) _____

9) _____

10) _____

11) _____

12) _____

<u>Day 1</u>

Today's Date: _____

What I did today: _____

_____

_____

_____

_____

What I liked best about today: _____

_____

_____

_____

NEW

TO ME!

Something new I tried:_____

_____

_____

_____

Today's weather: _____

<u>Day 1</u>

A fun thing that happened today was:

_____

_____

_____

_____

A drawing about my day:

Neat things I saw today: _____

_____

_____

_____

<u>Day 2</u>

Today's Date: _____

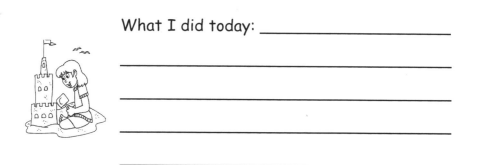

What I did today: _____

_____

_____

_____

_____

What I liked best about today: _____

_____

_____

_____

Something new I tried:_____

NEW

TO ME! —————————————————

_____

Today's weather: _____   <u>**Day 2**</u>

A fun thing that happened today was:

_____

_____

_____

_____

A drawing about my day:

Neat things I saw today: _____

_____

_____

_____

Day 3

Today's Date: _____

What I did today: _____
_____
_____
_____
_____

What I liked best about today: _____
_____
_____
_____

Something new I tried:_____

NEW
TO ME!
_____
_____
_____

Today's weather: _____

Day 3

A fun thing that happened today was:

_____

_____

_____

_____

A drawing about my day:

Neat things I saw today: _____

_____

_____

_____

<u>Day 4</u>

Today's Date: _____

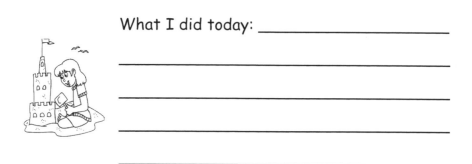

What I did today: _____

_____

_____

_____

_____

What I liked best about today: _____

_____

_____

_____

NEW

TO ME!

Something new I tried:_____

_____

_____

_____

Today's weather: _____ <u>Day 4</u>

A fun thing that happened today was:

_____

_____

_____

_____

A drawing about my day:

Neat things I saw today: _____

_____

_____

_____

Day 5

Today's Date: _____

What I did today: _____

_____

_____

_____

_____

What I liked best about today: _____

_____

_____

_____

NEW TO ME!

Something new I tried:_____

_____

_____

_____

Today's weather: _____

<u>Day 5</u>

A fun thing that happened today was:

_____

_____

_____

_____

A drawing about my day:

Neat things I saw today: _____

_____

_____

_____

<u>Day 6</u>

Today's Date: _____

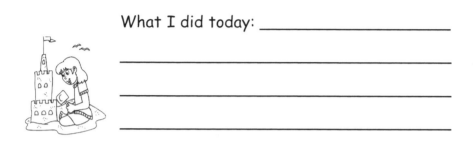

What I did today: _____

_____

_____

_____

_____

What I liked best about today: _____

_____

_____

_____

NEW TO ME!

Something new I tried:_____

_____

_____

_____

Today's weather: _____   <u>Day 6</u>

A fun thing that happened today was:

_____

_____

_____

_____

A drawing about my day:

Neat things I saw today: _____

_____

_____

_____

Day 7

Today's Date: _____

What I did today: _____

_____

_____

_____

_____

What I liked best about today: _____

_____

_____

_____

NEW
TO ME!

Something new I tried:_____

_____

_____

_____

Today's weather: _____   **Day 7**

A fun thing that happened today was:

_____

_____

_____

_____

A drawing about my day:

Neat things I saw today: _____

_____

_____

_____

<u>Day 8</u>

Today's Date: _____

What I did today: _____

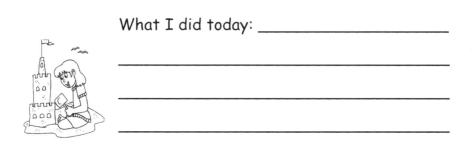

_____

_____

_____

_____

What I liked best about today: _____

_____

_____

_____

Something new I tried:_____

NEW

_____

TO ME! _____

_____

Today's weather: _____

Day 8

A fun thing that happened today was:

_____

_____

_____

_____

A drawing about my day:

Neat things I saw today: _____

_____

_____

_____

Day 9

Today's Date: _____

What I did today: _____
_____
_____
_____
_____

What I liked best about today: _____
_____
_____
_____

NEW
TO ME!

Something new I tried:_____
_____
_____
_____

Today's weather: _____

Day 9

A fun thing that happened today was:

_____

_____

_____

_____

A drawing about my day:

Neat things I saw today: _____

_____

_____

_____

<u>Day 10</u>

Today's Date: _____

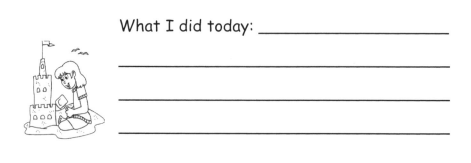

What I did today: _____

_____

_____

_____

_____

What I liked best about today: _____

_____

_____

_____

Something new I tried:_____

NEW

TO ME!

_____

_____

_____

Today's weather: _____

Day 10

A fun thing that happened today was:

_____

_____

_____

_____

A drawing about my day:

Neat things I saw today: _____

_____

_____

_____

My new friends!

(People I met while on my trip!)

Name: _____

Address: _____

City: _____ State _____ Zip _____

Email Address: _____

Other info: _____

Name: _____

Address: _____

City: _____ State _____ Zip _____

Email Address: _____

Other info: _____

Name: _____

Address: _____

City: _____ State _____ Zip _____

Email Address: _____

Other info: _____

Things I bought to remember this trip:

Item: Price

_____ $ _____

_____ $ _____

_____ $ _____

_____ $ _____

_____ $ _____

_____ $ _____

Reflection:

Use this area to write anything about your trip that you didn't write down already. Did your trip go the way you expected it to? Re-read your expectations and compare.

_____

_____

_____

_____

_____

_____

_____

_____

Other memories I want to remember!

(Tape or glue tickets, photos, postcards, and other things here to remember your trip! Or you can write more about your adventures. It's up to you!)

Other memories I want to remember!

(Tape or glue tickets, photos, postcards, and other things here to remember your trip! Or you can write more about your adventures. It's up to you!)

Other memories I want to remember!

(Tape or glue tickets, photos, postcards, and other things here to remember your trip! Or you can write more about your adventures. It's up to you!)

Other memories I want to remember!

(Tape or glue tickets, photos, postcards, and other things here to remember
your trip! Or you can write more about your adventures. It's up to you!)

Other memories I want to remember!

(Tape or glue tickets, photos, postcards, and other things here to remember your trip! Or you can write more about your adventures. It's up to you!)

<u>Trip #3</u>

My trip to

_____

(Write where you went here)

Date: _____

(When did you go?)

Preparing for my trip

Where am I going?

_____

(Are you going to the beach, grandma's house, amusement park?)

How am I getting there?

_____

(Are you going by car, airplane, train, or boat?)

How far away is it?

_____

(How many miles is it from your home to your destination?)

Who is going?

_____

(Is your brother going along? What about mom, dad, grandma, or a friend?)

What I need to do before I leave:

(See page 3 for tips on what to put here. Check the box when you have completed or taken care of that item.)

☐ _____

☐ _____

☐ _____

☐ _____

☐ _____

☐ _____

☐ _____

☐ _____

☐ _____

☐ _____

☐ _____

☐ _____

☐ _____

☐ _____

Things I want to take with me:

(See page 3 for tips on what to put here. Check the box beside each item after it is packed. Don't forget your toothbrush!)

☐ _____

☐ _____

☐ _____

☐ _____

☐ _____

☐ _____

☐ _____

☐ _____

☐ _____

☐ _____

☐ _____

☐ _____

☐ _____

☐ _____

What do I want to see and do on my trip?

(See page 3 for tips on what to put here.)

1) _____

2) _____

3) _____

4) _____

5) _____

6) _____

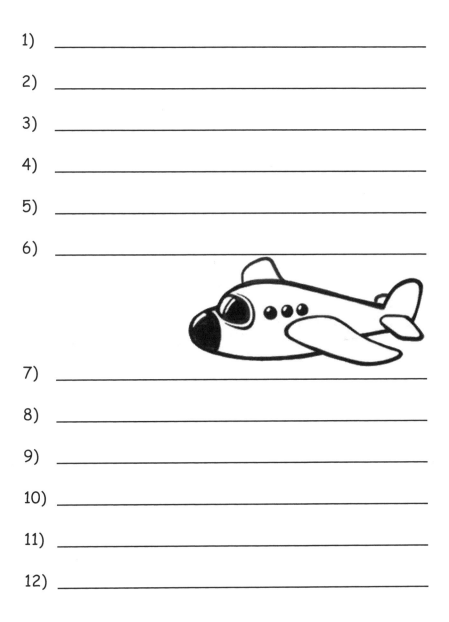

7) _____

8) _____

9) _____

10) _____

11) _____

12) _____

Who to send postcards to:

(Show them you care by sending a note!)

Post Card

Place Stamp Here

Name: _____

Address: _____

City: _____ State _____ Zip _____

Name: _____

Address: _____

City: _____ State _____ Zip _____

Name: _____

Address: _____

City: _____ State _____ Zip _____

Name: _____

Address: _____

City: _____ State _____ Zip _____

Expectations:

Use this area to write about what you think will happen on your trip. For example, do you expect to see family, animals, waves, windmills, dinosaurs, etc. Do you think you'll have fun or go to a fun restaurant? Try to predict the future and see how things turn out!

Do this part BEFORE leaving!

_____

_____

_____

_____

_____

Fun facts about where I'm going:

(Write a few interesting facts about where you are going.)

1) _____

2) _____

3) _____

4) _____

5) _____

6) _____

<u>Day 1</u>

Today's Date: _____

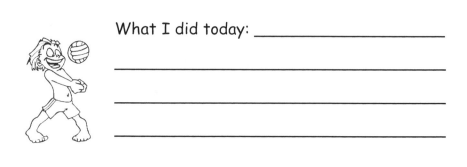

What I did today: _____

_____

_____

_____

_____

What I liked best about today: _____

_____

_____

_____

*Something new I tried:*_____

NEW

TO ME!

_____

_____

_____

Today's weather: _____

<u>Day 1</u>

A fun thing that happened today was:

_____

_____

_____

_____

A drawing about my day:

Neat things I saw today: _____

_____

_____

_____

<u>Day 2</u>

Today's Date: _____

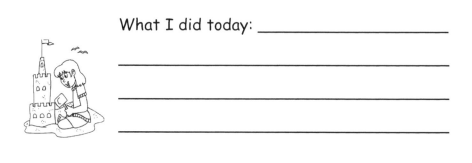

What I did today: _____

_____

_____

_____

_____

What I liked best about today: _____

_____

_____

_____

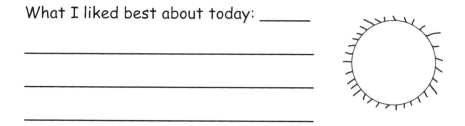

NEW TO ME!

Something new I tried:_____

_____

_____

_____

Today's weather: _____

Day 2

A fun thing that happened today was:

_____

_____

_____

_____

A drawing about my day:

Neat things I saw today: _____

_____

_____

_____

Day 3

Today's Date: _____

What I did today: _____

_____

_____

_____

_____

What I liked best about today: _____

_____

_____

_____

Something new I tried:_____

NEW

TO ME!

_____

_____

_____

Today's weather: _____

Day 3

A fun thing that happened today was:

_____

_____

_____

_____

A drawing about my day:

Neat things I saw today: _____

_____

_____

_____

Day 4

Today's Date: _____

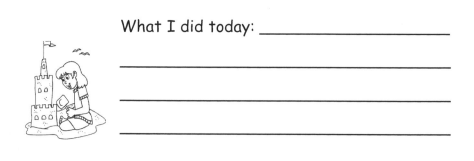

What I did today: _____

_____

_____

_____

_____

What I liked best about today: _____

_____

_____

_____

NEW
TO ME!

Something new I tried:_____

_____

_____

_____

Today's weather: _____   ## Day 4

A fun thing that happened today was:

_____

_____

_____

_____

A drawing about my day:

Neat things I saw today: _____

_____

_____

_____

Day 5

Today's Date: _____

What I did today: _____

_____

_____

_____

_____

What I liked best about today: _____

_____

_____

_____

NEW TO ME!

Something new I tried: _____

_____

_____

_____

Today's weather: _____

<u>Day 5</u>

A fun thing that happened today was:

_____

_____

_____

_____

A drawing about my day:

Neat things I saw today: _____

_____

_____

_____

<u>Day 6</u>

Today's Date: _____

What I did today: _____

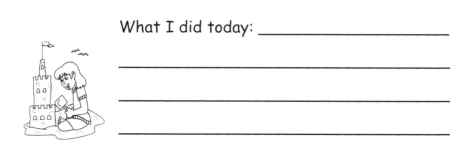

_____

_____

_____

_____

What I liked best about today: _____

_____

_____

_____

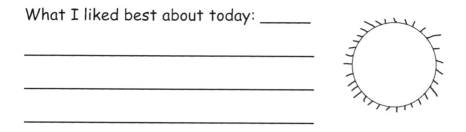

NEW
TO ME!

Something new I tried:_____

_____

_____

_____

Today's weather: _____

Day 6

A fun thing that happened today was:

_____

_____

_____

_____

A drawing about my day:

Neat things I saw today: _____

_____

_____

_____

Day 7

Today's Date: _____

What I did today: _____

_____

_____

_____

_____

What I liked best about today: _____

_____

_____

_____

NEW

TO ME!

Something new I tried:_____

_____

_____

_____

Today's weather: _____

Day 7

A fun thing that happened today was:

_____

_____

_____

_____

A drawing about my day:

Neat things I saw today: _____

_____

_____

_____

Day 8

Today's Date: _____

What I did today: _____

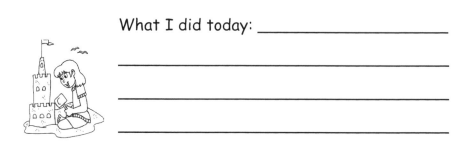

_____

_____

_____

_____

What I liked best about today: _____

_____

_____

_____

Something new I tried:_____

NEW

TO ME!

_____

_____

_____

Today's weather: _____

A fun thing that happened today was:

_____

_____

_____

_____

A drawing about my day:

Neat things I saw today: _____

_____

_____

_____

Day 9

Today's Date: _____

What I did today: _____

_____

_____

_____

_____

What I liked best about today: _____

_____

_____

_____

NEW

TO ME!

Something new I tried:_____

_____

_____

_____

Today's weather: _____   <u>Day 9</u>

A fun thing that happened today was:

_____

_____

_____

_____

A drawing about my day:

Neat things I saw today: _____

_____

_____

_____

<u>Day 10</u>

Today's Date: _____

What I did today: _____

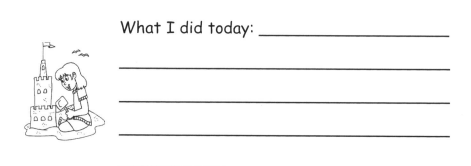

_____

_____

_____

_____

What I liked best about today: _____

_____

_____

_____

Something new I tried:_____

NEW
TO ME!

_____

_____

_____

Today's weather: _____   <u>Day 10</u>

A fun thing that happened today was:

_____

_____

_____

_____

A drawing about my day:

Neat things I saw today: _____

_____

_____

_____

My new friends!

(People I met while on my trip!)

Name: _____

Address: _____

City: _____ State _____ Zip _____

Email Address: _____

Other info: _____

Name: _____

Address: _____

City: _____ State _____ Zip _____

Email Address: _____

Other info: _____

Name: _____

Address: _____

City: _____ State _____ Zip _____

Email Address: _____

Other info: _____

Things I bought to remember this trip:

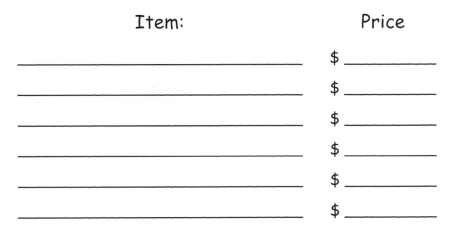

Item:	Price
_____	$ _____
_____	$ _____
_____	$ _____
_____	$ _____
_____	$ _____
_____	$ _____

Reflection:

Use this area to write anything about your trip that you didn't write down already. Did your trip go the way you expected? Re-read your expectations and compare. Is this a trip you want to do again?

_____

_____

_____

_____

_____

_____

_____

_____

Other memories I want to remember!

(Tape or glue tickets, photos, postcards, and other things here to remember your trip! Or you can write more about your adventures. It's up to you!)

Other memories I want to remember!

(Tape or glue tickets, photos, postcards, and other things here to remember
your trip! Or you can write more about your adventures. It's up to you!)

Other memories I want to remember!

(Tape or glue tickets, photos, postcards, and other things here to remember your trip! Or you can write more about your adventures. It's up to you!)

Other memories I want to remember!

(Tape or glue tickets, photos, postcards, and other things here to remember your trip! Or you can write more about your adventures. It's up to you!)

Other memories I want to remember!

(Tape or glue tickets, photos, postcards, and other things here to remember your trip! Or you can write more about your adventures. It's up to you!)

Fun Travel Games!

Play these games with your family on your trip. They are great no matter where you are!

Odds or Evens

Two players pick either "odds" or "evens." They then make a fist, shake it, say "one, two, three, shoot" and stick out either one or two fingers. If the total is an odd number then "odds" wins. If it is an even number, "evens" wins.

I Spy

One person starts by finding something inside or outside the vehicle. They then describe the item (or person or animal) by giving everyone else clues. Whoever guesses what it is first gets to find the next item.

My Favorite Things

Go around the car and ask each person their favorite color. Then have everyone think of another "favorite" question to ask the group. Be creative and don't forget to include the driver!

Would You Rather

Ask each other questions of decisions you hope you'd never have to make.

For example: "Would you rather have your nose where your ears are or have your arms on backwards?"

End Game

Player 1 spots a word on a road sign, billboard, restaurant, etc. Player 2 then has to spot a word that begins with the last letter of Player 1's word.

For example: If Player 1 sees the word "Burger," Player 2 must find a word that starts with "R."

License Plate Lingo

Look at the license plate of a passing car. Try to come up with a phrase using the letters on that car's license plate.

For example: If the car's license plate says AIW 2011, the first person to call out a logical phrase such as "All I Want" or "Anyone Is Welcome" wins.

Spelling Bee

See who can spell the most words out loud correctly.
Choose words that fit with the vocabulary level of each
person playing. Pick harder words for older kids and
easier words for the younger players. Be sure to ask the
adults too!

Don't Say "Um"

Pick a topic and go around the car and see if each person
can talk about the topic for 20 seconds without using the
words "um," "hmm," "let's see," or without making any long
pauses. It is harder than it sounds!

License Plate Search

Play by yourself or in teams. Watch passing cars and try
to find as many different license plates as you can. See
if you can find all 50 states!

Word Factory

Write down a short 2 or 3 word phrase and see how many different words you can create using the letters of those words. The person who can create the most words wins.

For example: See how many words you can find by using the letters in "Family Vacation" – Fan, Van, Cat, Mat, and so on.

- -

Find these and over 140 games, riddles and tongue twisters in "Are We There Yet?"
ISBN: 978-1463785444

3266704R00063

Made in the USA
San Bernardino, CA
20 July 2013